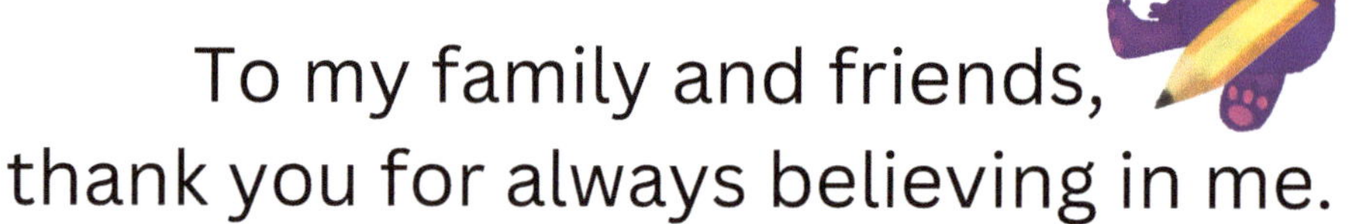

To my family and friends,
thank you for always believing in me.

Library of Congress Catalog Card Number: 2024915694

ISBN 979-8-218-32933-4

Trinity Ink Press LLC
San Diego, California

Visit us at www.trinityinkpress.com for more information.

Not Today, Math Monster

By Heather Dahl-Hansen

Illustrated by Angélica Baldit

"Done! You can give me my A+ now!"
said Stella as she pictured her teacher putting an A+
on her worksheet with his shiny golden stamp.

"Are you sure you're ready to turn it in?" asked Mr. Trust,
"I just handed you your math worksheet."

"Umm…I think so," said Stella.

All of the sudden a tiny monster appeared on her worksheet.

"I'm Crazy Baby Pants!" he yelled as he danced wildly.

There were 18 donuts,
and a cat ate 5 of them.
How many were left?

$$\begin{array}{r} 18 \\ -\ 5 \\ \hline 12 \end{array}$$

Where did he even come from? wondered Stella and why is he named Crazy Baby Pants? He wasn't even wearing pants!
HISTORY
BIOLOGY
MATH

Then Crazy Baby Pants grabbed a pencil and started changing some of her answers.

"Not today, math monster!" said Stella as she asked Mr. Trust a very important question, "Can I check my own work?"

"Of course," he said, as he handed her the answer key.

"You're going down Crazy Baby Pants!" said Stella as she went back to her desk and started checking her work.

She found an incorrect answer for problem #5. The answer key showed the correct answer was 14, but she had 41 on her paper. What happened? thought Stella.

She went back and checked the problem: 11 + 3 = 41.
She realized the number in her answer was reversed!
Nice try, math monster thought Stella as she corrected
her answer to 14.

As she continued checking her work, Crazy Baby Pants tried to jump onto her pencil.

"Not today, math monster!" said Stella as she flicked him across the room.

"Ahhh!" he screamed as he landed in the hamster cage.

"Yummy!" squeaked Nibbles,
the fluffy class hamster.

The next few problems were correct, but then she found an incorrect answer to a word problem: There were 18 donuts, and a cat ate 5 of them. How many were left?

On her worksheet, she had written 12, but that didn't seem quite right. Maybe I should draw it out, thought Stella.

She drew the donuts and started to cross them out.

Then, Crazy Baby Pants ran across her paper to get the donuts. She quickly crossed out five and counted the rest. *Thirteen! The answer is thirteen!* thought Stella as she corrected her answer.

She grabbed Crazy Baby Pants and tossed him in a cup of glue. "Not today, math monster!" Stella said as she watched him fall into a bin of art supplies.

Now the tiny monster was covered in glitter, jewels, and feathers.
"You look like a sparkly chicken!" she laughed.

As Stella corrected her last math problem, Crazy Baby Pants disappeared into an explosion of rainbow glitter.

This time Stella felt confident when she turned in her math worksheet.

Mr. Trust reviewed her work and brought out the shiny gold A+ stamp she had been waiting for all week!

"But I had a few wrong answers when I first turned in my worksheet," said Stella.

"That's ok," said Mr. Trust, "You went back, figured out what you did wrong, and corrected your mistakes. That was a very smart choice!

From that day forward, Stella took her time, checked her work, and learned from her mistakes…ultimately defeating Crazy Baby Pants!

Stella wondered if Crazy Baby Pants would ever return, and if he did, she knew what to say:

NOT MATH

TODAY
MONSTER